I0797359

EMERGING TECHNOLOGY

NANOMEDICINE

Martin Gitlin and Alexis Roumanis

LIGHTBOX

Go to **www.openlightbox.com** and enter this book's unique code.

ACCESS CODE

LBXR3239

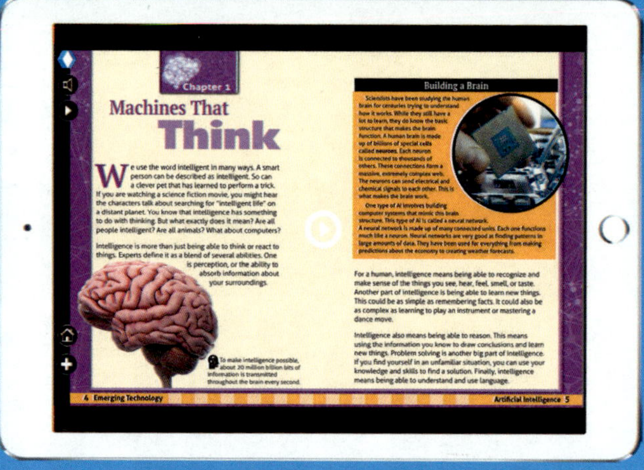

Lightbox is an all-inclusive digital solution for the teaching and learning of curriculum topics in an original, groundbreaking way. Lightbox is based on National Curriculum Standards.

STANDARD FEATURES OF LIGHTBOX

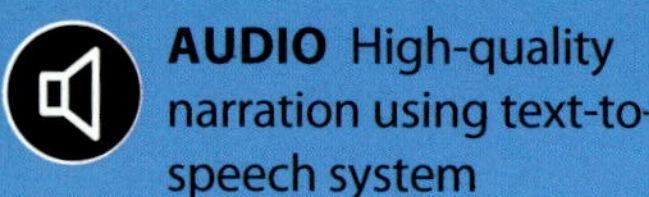

AUDIO High-quality narration using text-to-speech system

ACTIVITIES Printable PDFs that can be emailed and graded

SLIDESHOWS Pictorial overviews of key concepts

VIDEOS Embedded high-definition video clips

WEBLINKS Curated links to external, child-safe resources

TRANSPARENCIES Step-by-step layering of maps, diagrams, charts, and timelines

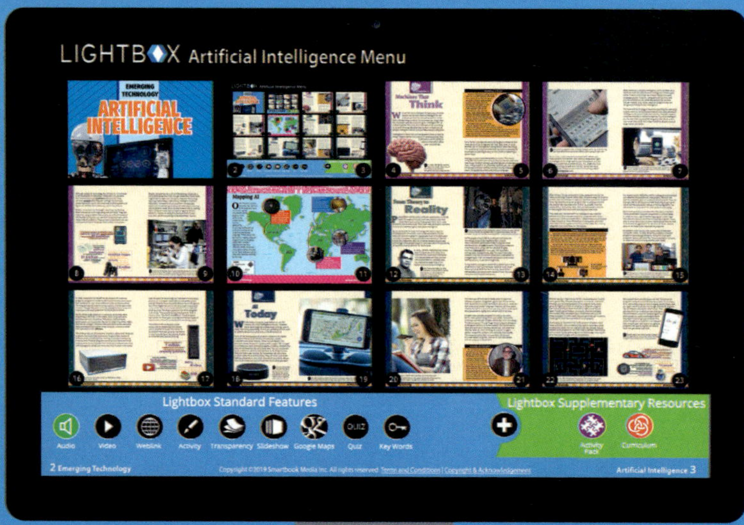

INTERACTIVE MAPS Interactive maps and aerial satellite imagery

QUIZZES Ten multiple choice questions that are automatically graded and emailed for teacher assessment

KEY WORDS Matching key concepts to their definitions

Contents

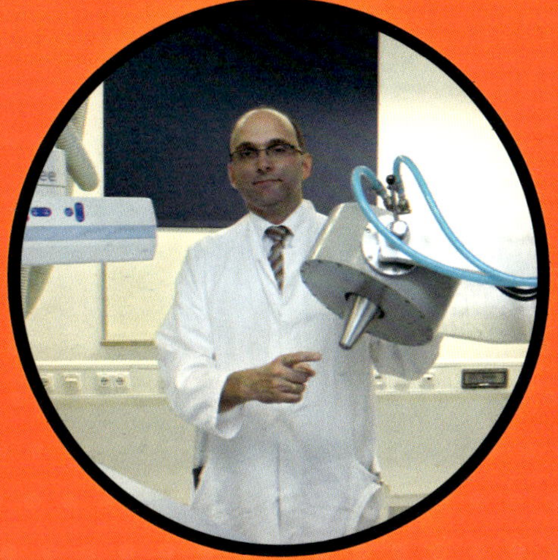

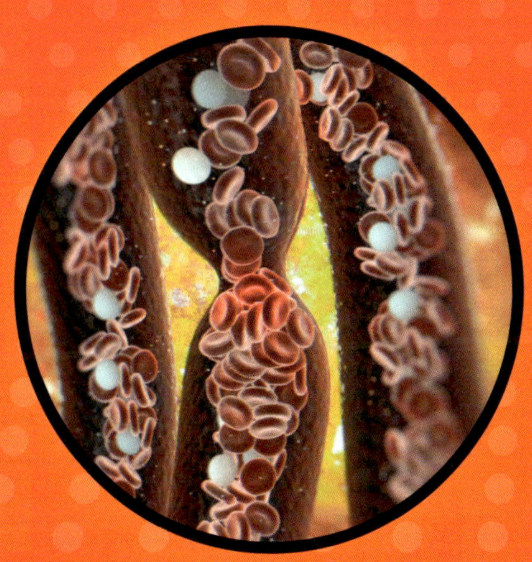

Tiny Treatments

It is late summer of 1966. Americans flock to theaters to watch a science-fiction film titled *Fantastic Voyage*. The plot revolves around a scientist named Jan Benes. He has perfected a secret formula that shrinks people and objects down to miniature size. Later, Benes strikes his head and suffers a blood clot in his brain. He has only a short time to live.

A group of scientists is shrunk down using Benes's secret formula. They must travel through his body, remove the clot in his brain, and get out before he dies. They are placed in a tiny submarine and injected into his bloodstream. And so begins the "fantastic voyage." The explorers travel into Benes's heart, through his inner ear, and into his brain. Once the clot is removed, they have only six minutes to exit the body. In the end, they save Benes.

In Fantastic Voyage, the shrunken scientists face realistic challenges such as turbulence in the bloodstream and fighting off the immune system of the patient.

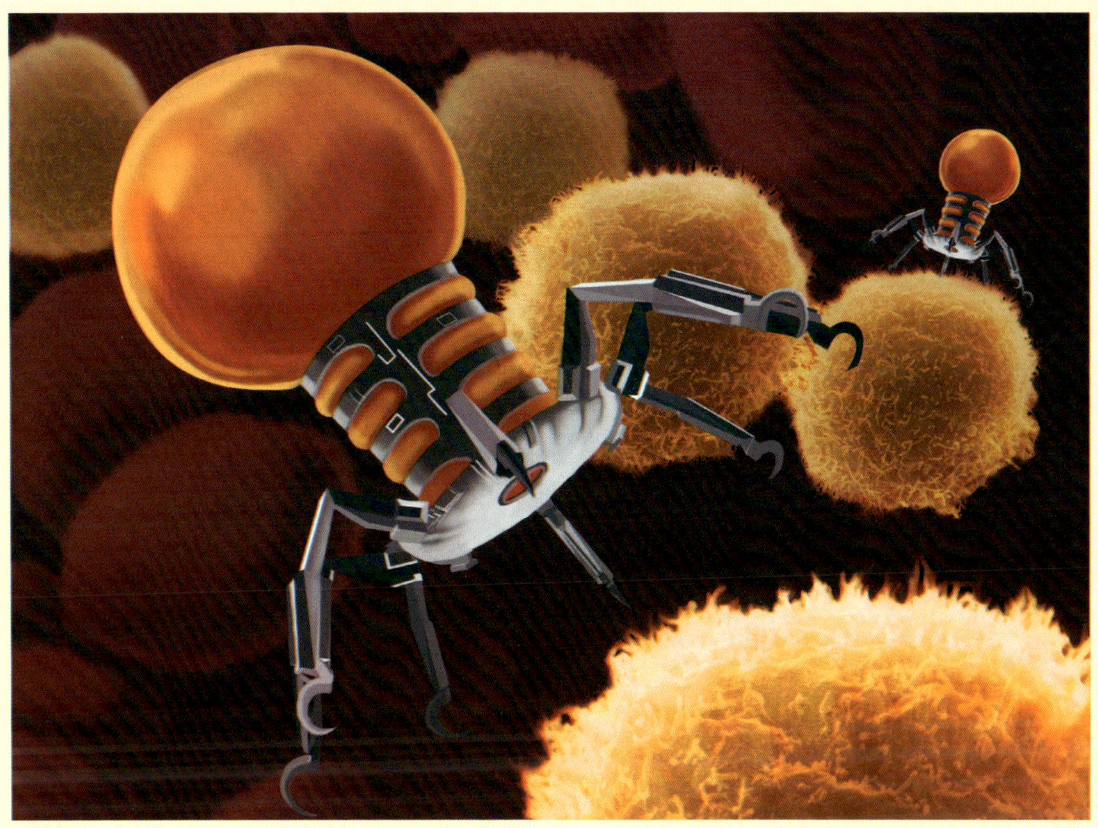

The devices used in nanomedicine can change in size depending on their use. The smallest devices would be needed to enter the bloodstream, while devices at least 100 times larger could be used to repair tissue damage.

Even today, the idea of tiny people traveling inside a human body to cure an illness might seem crazy. But more than 50 years after *Fantastic Voyage* hit theaters, a similar way of treating health problems has become a reality.

Welcome to the world of nanomedicine. The prefix *nano* refers to things that are very small. Nanomedicine is the use of incredibly small devices to treat illnesses inside the body. Just how tiny are these devices? Believe it or not, they are much smaller than the width of a hair! Yet despite their tiny size, they have a lot of power. They could even be used to save lives.

The Artistic Side of Richard Feynman

Richard Feynman was a Nobel Prize–winning physicist who predicted the coming of nanotechnology. But he was also a man of many other talents. His sense of humor made his lectures and books highly entertaining. He was also an artist whose primary focus was on drawing. A collection of his artwork was published in 1995 in a book titled *The Art of Richard P. Feynman: Images by a Curious Character*. Feynman also became quite adept at playing the bongo drums. He died in 1988 at the age of 69.

Nanomedicine is part of a larger field called nanotechnology. Nanotechnology deals with devices that range in size from 1 nanometer (0.00000000328 feet) to 100 nanometers. The concept of nanotechnology extends back to 1959. That is when renowned physicist Richard Feynman spoke at an American Physical Society meeting. Feynman described a future in which **atoms** and **molecules** would be manipulated one by one using precise instruments.

Feynman claimed that tools could be built to create and operate even smaller tools. This process would be repeated. Eventually the tools would be tiny enough to work on individual atoms and molecules.

The idea of working with devices on such a small scale gained credibility over time. Scientific breakthroughs resulted in greater knowledge of nanotechnology. Such learning led to new ideas about its potential benefits in the world of medicine.

The uses of nanomedicine we are likely to see in the near future would have once read like a science fiction story. For example, nanorobots placed in the bloodstream could warn of worsening illnesses or repair damaged cells. Machines planted in the body's nervous system could monitor a person's brain waves.

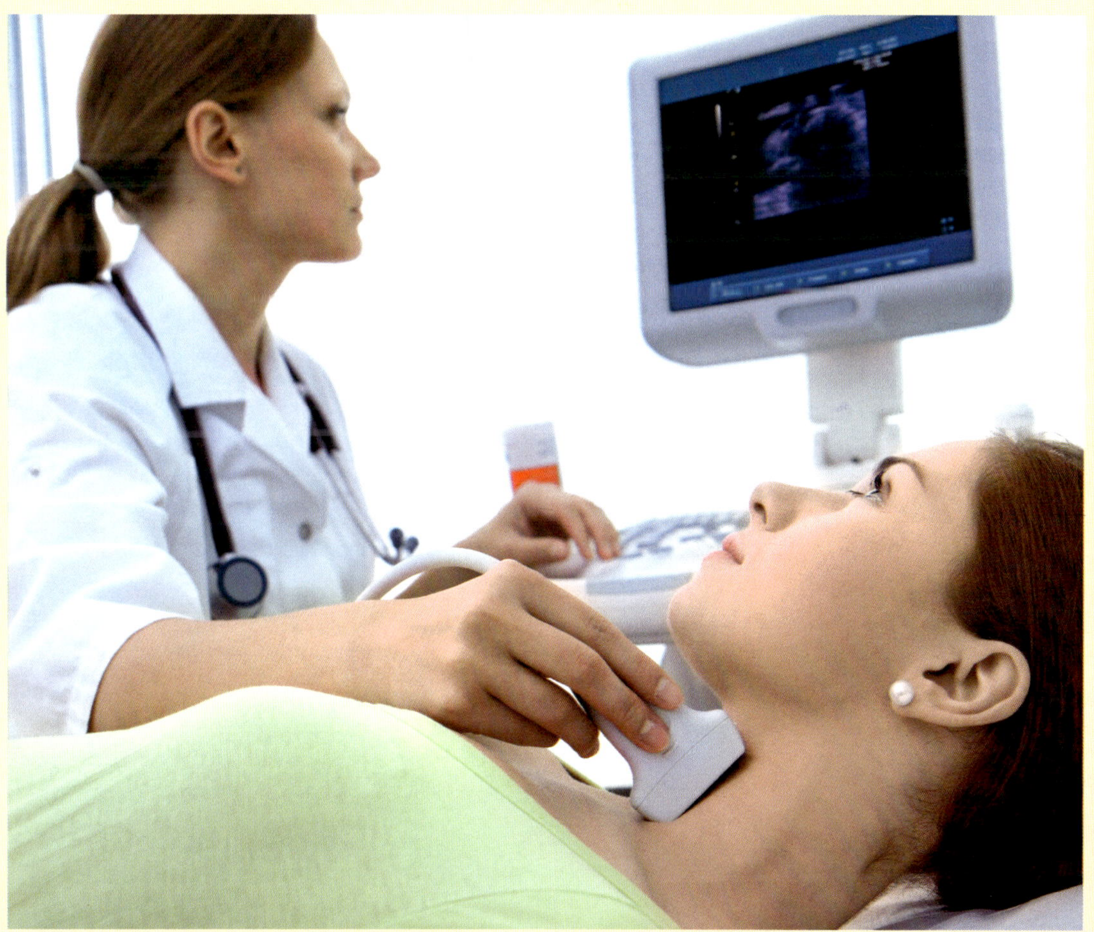

To receive messages from nanorobots, each nanorobot would relay sound-wave signals to one central location inside the body. Doctors would use an ultrasound probe to monitor this location to receive messages.

Today's researchers believe that nanotechnology can be applied to many different areas of medicine. Among them is the transport of needed drugs to diseased cells. Another potential use of nanomedicine is therapy. This might involve using tiny sponges that travel through the body to remove **toxins** from the bloodstream.

Nanomedicine researchers have also focused on detecting diseases. For example, they have used tiny electronic devices to spot cancer cells. The hope is that this method can eventually be used to find cancer before it has a chance to spread.

Nanomedicine **cancer treatments** could save about **600,000 lives** in the United States each year.

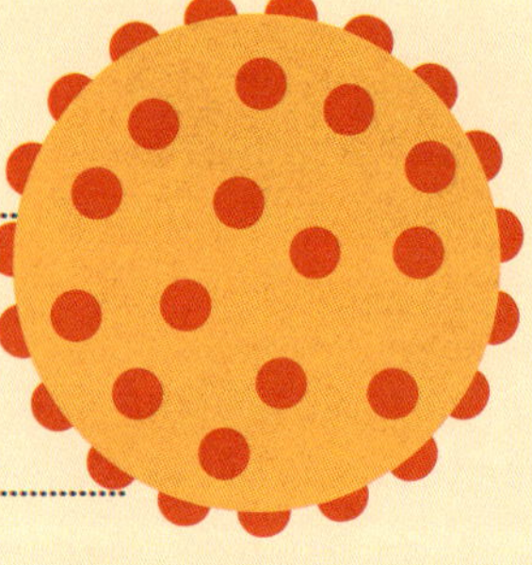

The nanomedicine market is expected to be worth **$350 billion** by **2025**.

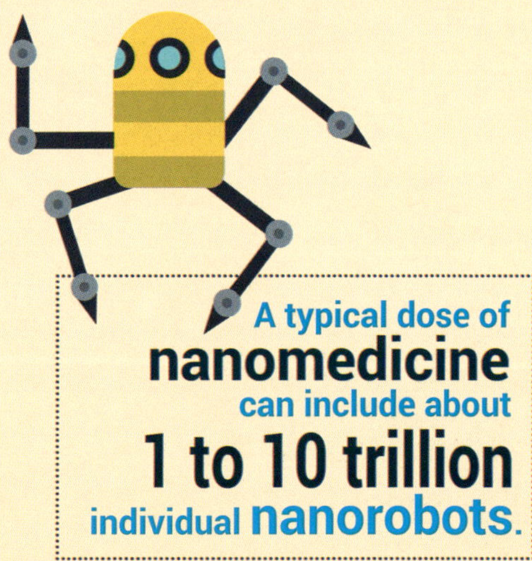

A typical dose of **nanomedicine** can include about **1 to 10 trillion** individual **nanorobots**.

Other studies target the early elimination of **bacterial** infections. Nanomedicine can be used to destroy bacteria in the body within minutes instead of requiring weeks of treatment.

Much work must be done to relieve suffering and save lives. It is hoped that nanomedicine can wipe out or at least weaken some of the world's deadliest diseases. The most critical of all is cancer, which is the leading cause of death in the United States. It remains to be seen if nanomedicine can help cure such diseases. But this remarkable technology certainly has the potential to aid in many types of treatment and has already begun to make a difference.

By using nanobots to discover cancer, bacterial infections, and other diseases earlier, doctors will be able to offer patients more treatment options and better odds of survival.

Mapping Nanomedicine

During the 20th century, the science of nanomedicine has expanded considerably. Experts have found many different uses for nanomedicine to fight various diseases, and to deliver medicine to specific locations in the human body. Discover more about advancements in the field of nanomedicine and the universities and research centers where they take place by looking at the map.

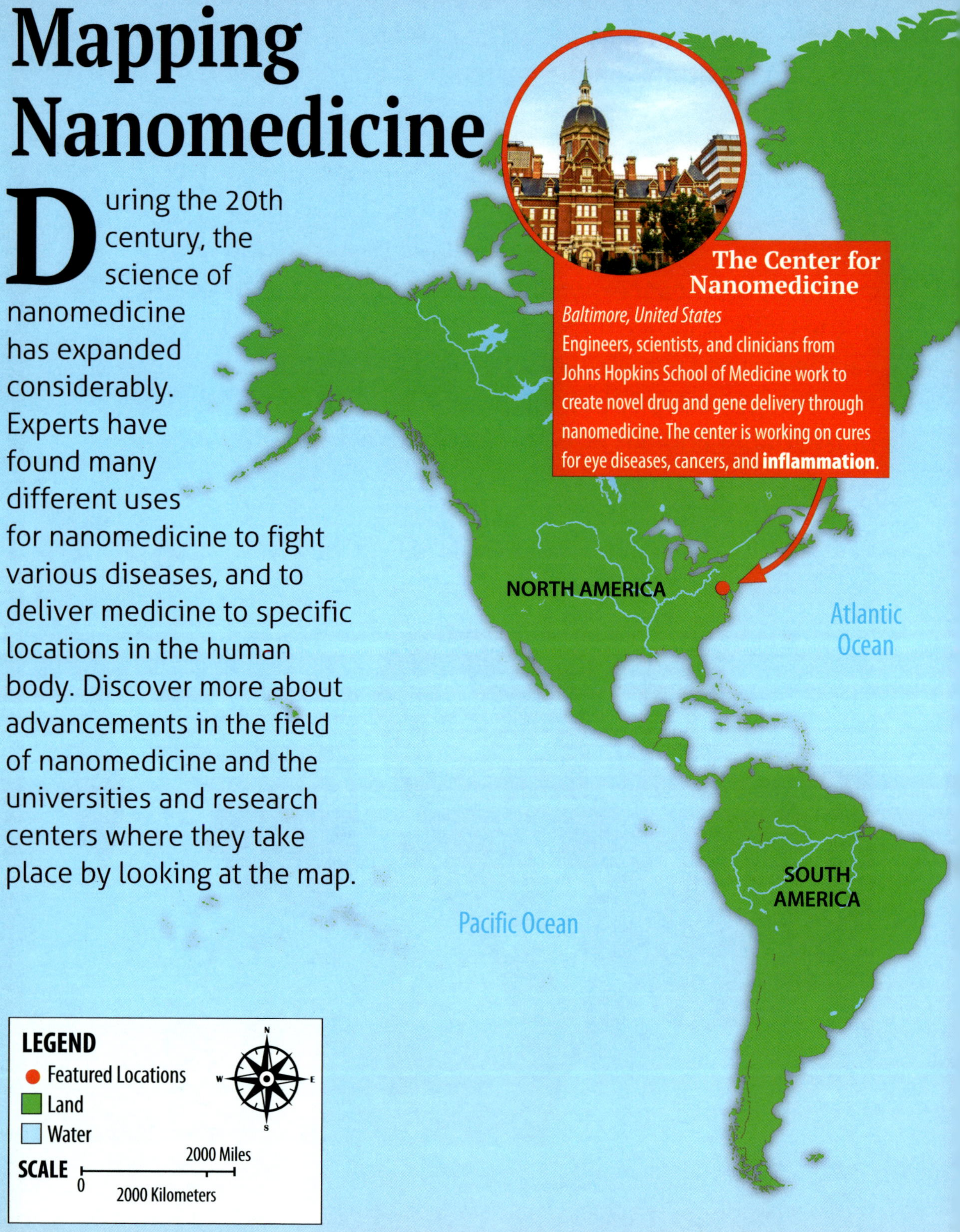

The Center for Nanomedicine

Baltimore, United States

Engineers, scientists, and clinicians from Johns Hopkins School of Medicine work to create novel drug and gene delivery through nanomedicine. The center is working on cures for eye diseases, cancers, and **inflammation**.

NORTH AMERICA

SOUTH AMERICA

Atlantic Ocean

Pacific Ocean

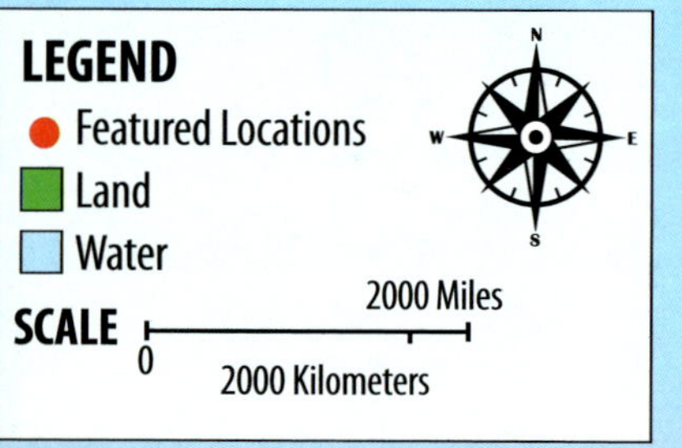

Friedrich-Alexander University

Erlangen, Germany

Friedrich-Alexander University uses experimental nanoparticles to fight cancer. Nanoparticles that are combined with medicine are placed into **tumors** using a powerful magnet.

European Centre for Nanomedicine

Milan, Italy

The European Centre for Nanomedicine is developing solutions for the prevention, diagnosis, and treatment of diseases. It is partnered with universities, companies, and medical centers to work on treatments for cancer, organ failure, and various diseases.

University of Oxford

Oxford, United Kingdom

The University of Oxford offers students education in scientific, regulatory, clinical, and commercial aspects of nanotechnology in healthcare. The program specifically helps working professionals to gain a greater understanding of nanomedicine.

Chapter 2

Drug Delivery

It is the year 2043. A woman has been diagnosed with brain cancer. But she is lucky. A carbon nanotube placed in her bloodstream spotted the cancer cells at an early stage. Earlier in the 21st century, the disease might not have been detected until it was too late to save her.

Even in 2043, there is still no true cure for cancer. Patients continue to need **chemotherapy** to survive. However, nanomedicine will save this woman's life. The days of exhausting traditional chemotherapy treatments are over. Instead, nanoparticles targeting diseased cells will be placed inside her bloodstream. They will deliver drugs directly to the cancer and destroy it. The woman is expected to live a long and healthy life.

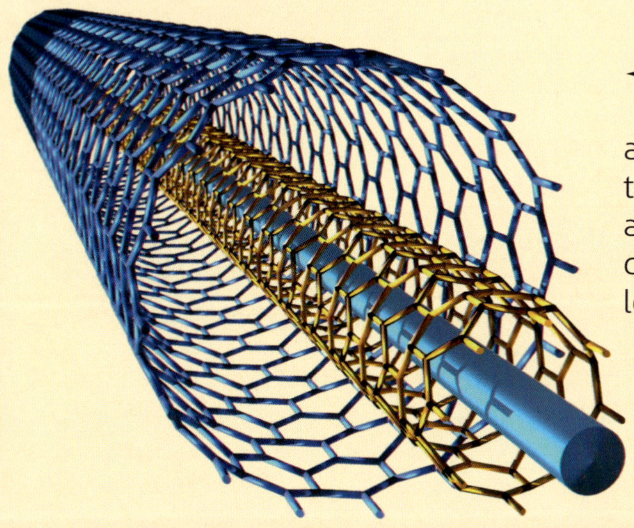

Carbon nanotubes are exceptionally strong, allowing long tubes to maintain their strength. This strength allows carbon nanotubes to deliver nanoparticles to a target location in the body.

Let's Play Buckyball!

Perhaps the most fun word associated with nanomedicine is buckyball. Buckyball is a common term for a carbon molecule shaped like a soccer ball. A buckyball consists of 60 carbon atoms. Scientists have proven buckyballs to be effective in the fight against allergies. They can block allergic responses in human cells.

Researchers have begun the process of harnessing the properties of buckyballs to develop new allergy drugs and other tools. Many millions of people would welcome relief from allergies that cause sneezing, itching, runny noses, and watery eyes.

Research and development of drug delivery is the most advanced area of nanomedicine. Particles engineered to be attracted to diseased cells result in speedy and direct treatment. Nanomedicine avoids damaging healthy cells by traveling directly to those that are diseased. It also boasts the ability to control its release time. The drugs are not dispensed until they reach the unhealthy cells.

Cancer patients have often undergone **radiation** treatment in addition to chemotherapy to fight their disease. Nanomedicine combined with radiation can destroy cancer cells faster and more effectively than traditional radiation treatments. Nanoparticles that enter tumors absorb the radiation and heat up enough to kill the infected cells.

This all adds up to a promising trend in the battle against cancer. Companies have tested nanodelivery radiation drugs in clinical trials. They are seeking final approval for use on cancer patients.

Cancer is not the only disease studied by nanomedicine scientists. Tests on drug delivery for brain injuries have also yielded promising results. They have shown that nanoparticles can be used to send drugs more effectively to damaged brain tissue than traditional methods.

Increasing Appetites

Nanotechnology researchers have already produced drugs to treat many problems. Among these medications is Megace ES, which is designed to stimulate appetite in patients suffering from conditions such as anorexia. Anorexia is an emotional disorder that causes people to develop an obsessive desire to lose weight. Extreme weight loss has also decreased the quality of life for people who have diseases such as AIDS.

Early research showed that Megace ES dramatically increased food intake in test patients. People were able to quickly gain weight and return to healthy conditions. Megace ES nanocrystals can be taken by simply swallowing them. They dissolve and begin working much faster than other drugs that affect appetite. Megace ES reduces many of the symptoms associated with rapid weight loss, including the following.

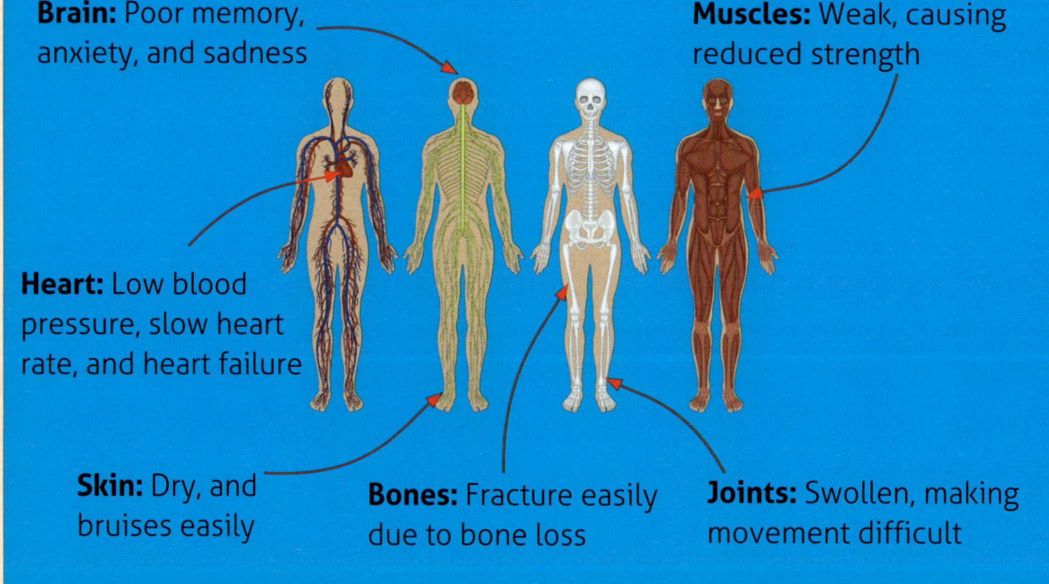

Researchers have even experimented with using nanoparticles to clear out blood clots like the one suffered by Jan Benes in *Fantastic Voyage*. These devices release drugs by sheer force. That force is needed when passing through a blood vessel that is blocked by a clot. When the nanoparticles collide with clots, the drugs inside them cause the clots to dissolve.

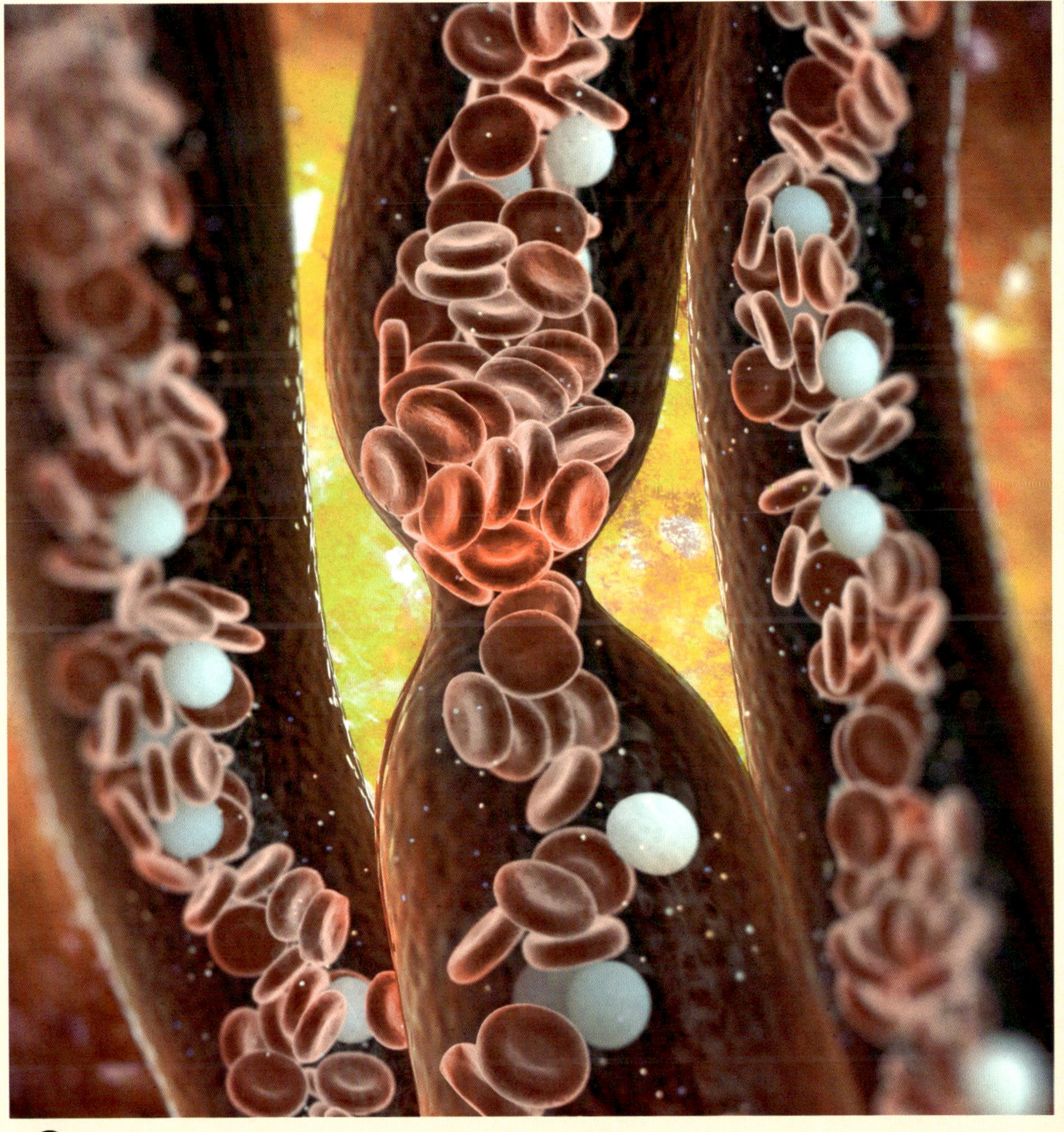

Blood clots prevent blood from flowing freely through a vessel. This can quickly lead to many other health complications as parts of the body do not receive enough blood to function correctly.

People who are afraid of shots can find hope in nanomedicine, as well. Researchers have worked on nanoparticles that can be swallowed. They pass through the lining of the intestines and into the bloodstream. This allows patients to get the necessary medication into their blood without using needles.

Researchers are working on bacteria-resistant nanoparticles made from silver that can be swallowed. Silver nanoparticles are also being used as a coating on clothing, bandages, and keyboards to stop bacteria from forming.

Nanomedicine will likely not end the need for surgery to treat certain conditions, but it can help make operations easier. Tiny surgical instruments and robots could be created and used in microsurgery on any part of the body. The equipment would be small and precise enough to target only damaged areas.

Nanomedicine would allow surgeons to keep their hands free. Rather than holding the surgical instruments, they would use computers to control the nanobots. Miniature cameras would give them a close-up of the targeted area inside the body. This could reduce the chance of making mistakes.

Since 1995, about **30 nanoparticle drugs** have been made available for public use in the **United States.**

Electron microscopes are used in **nanomedicine** to magnify things more than **500,000** times.

Nanorobots used in **surgeries** could help to clot, or harden, blood about **1,000 times** faster than the body could naturally.

Chapter 3

Therapeutic Nanomedicine

Imagine you walk around in pain all day. You feel it in your feet. You feel it in your hands. You feel it in your legs. You have been diagnosed with arthritis. It is a disease that results in stiffness and inflammation in the joints. For the many people affected by the disease, it can be agonizing.

One day, you complain to your friend about it. He is sympathetic. But he has his own problem. He reveals that he has been stricken with multiple sclerosis. This disease affects the brain and spinal cord while causing numbness, blurred vision, and weakness. He worries that he might lose the ability to walk.

The myelin sheath, a protective layer surrounding some neurons, becomes damaged in multiple sclerosis patients.

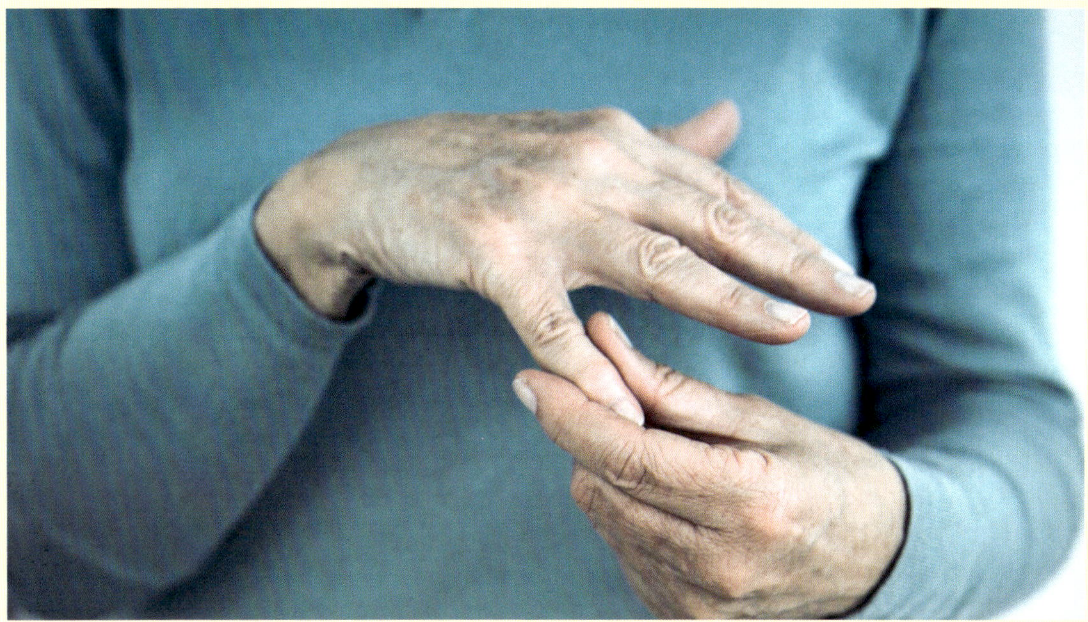

In the United States, about half of all people age 65 or older are diagnosed with some form of arthritis.

Yet you feel a sense of hope when you learn that nanomedicine might help find cures. You also discover that nanomedicine is already used in therapy to relieve pain associated with arthritis and multiple sclerosis. It is even hoped that nanomedicine can aid in wiping out these devastating ailments for good.

The most important potential benefit of nanomedicine in the treatment of arthritis is early detection. Conventional methods do not spot the disease until it is rather advanced. Nanoparticles allow doctors to easily see the differences between healthy and unhealthy tissue. They help create a high-resolution picture that highlights inflamed joints.

Nanoparticles can also help improve the potential success of certain drug treatments for arthritis. They can be created to reach tissues quickly and release drugs that reduce inflammation. Their precise targeting of infected areas decreases the amount of drugs needed to be effective. This lessens the risk of suffering side effects from the medication.

Currently, diabetes patients need a small sample of blood to test their blood-sugar levels. Scientists are working on ingestible nanomedicine that can track blood-sugar levels inside the body.

Advances in the treatment of multiple sclerosis bring encouragement, as well. Traditional therapy options have been limited for people suffering from this disease. They require repeated drug intake for long periods of time. However, drug delivery through nanomedicine promises to treat multiple sclerosis more efficiently.

Nanomedicine researchers seek to help those suffering from many other ailments, including diabetes. This disease occurs when blood sugar levels in the body are too high. Diabetes patients must inject **insulin** several times a day. These insulin treatments have made diabetes less of a threat than it once was. However, it remains the seventh-leading cause of death in the United States. Diabetes can lead to blindness and obesity. A recent increase in the disease among children has raised concern. Previously, it had mostly affected the elderly.

Research shows that nanoparticles can deliver insulin through the nose or be swallowed in pill form. Such methods of controlling diabetes are painless. They do not require surgery or injections. Another technique using nanomedicine allows insulin to be stored after it is injected into the skin. This would mean patients would not have to get injections as often as they do today.

Another troubling disease that often affects older people is Alzheimer's. This disease damages brain cells, resulting in a loss of memory and a failure to think clearly. Alzheimer's leads to an inability to function and eventually causes death. It has been estimated that it affects 30 million people worldwide. That number is predicted to double by the year 2050. Unfortunately, there has been little development in its diagnosis and therapy.

Fiction or Future?

A team of scientists in India has created a nanoparticle that can deliver drugs to stimulate growth of bone-forming cells. The method will be used to help those suffering from osteoporosis. Osteoporosis is a disease that weakens the bones. It mostly affects older people. Patients suffering from the disease feel pain even when bending over or coughing.

Previous osteoporosis treatments have only served to restrict further damage to patients' bones. They have not returned bone strength. However, the drugs carried by nanoparticles have proven effective in repairing weakened bones. This could help restore a better quality of life for many osteoporosis patients.

Nanoparticles could play a critical role in reversing Alzheimer's. They could break through what is known as the blood-brain barrier (BBB). The BBB is a physical fence made of cells protecting the brain from harmful substances in the blood. But it also prevents nearly all drugs from reaching the brain. Scientists have designed nanoparticles to cross the BBB and deliver treatment. The capacity to pass the BBB could also allow nanoparticles to help in the battle against Parkinson's disease. This disorder of the nervous system makes it hard for people to control their movements. While many treatments and surgical procedures to battle Parkinson's are available, their benefits are not permanent. Nanomedicine could assist those with Parkinson's in much the same way it could aid victims of Alzheimer's.

Infectious diseases are another problem that nanomedicine could help solve. These illnesses can quickly spread from person to person and affect huge numbers of people. One well-known example is Ebola, a virus that spread from West Africa and has killed thousands.

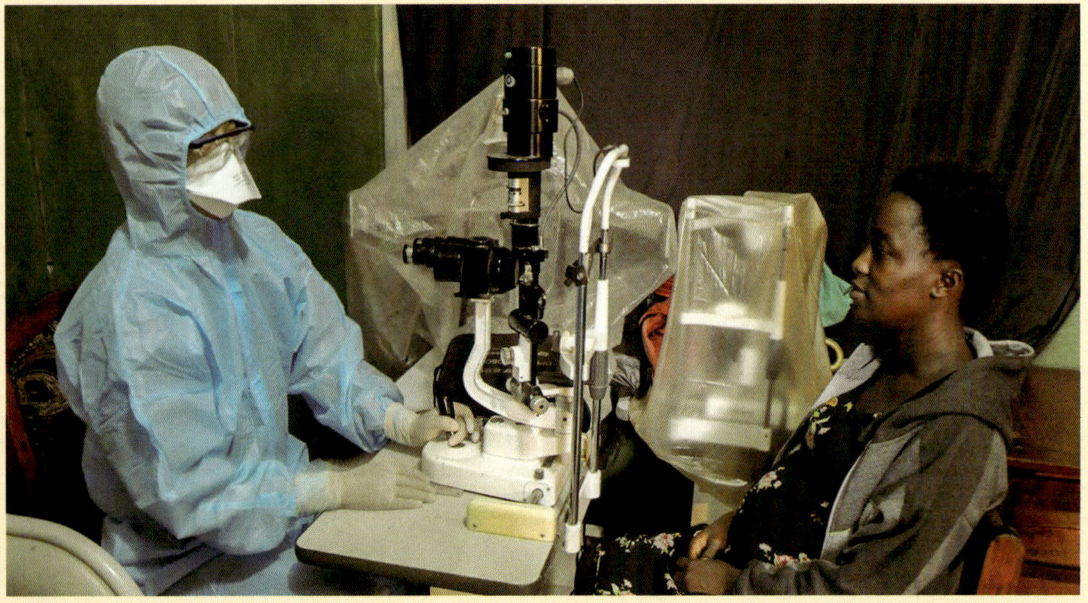

Ebola can spread between people very easily. This means health care workers must be extremely careful to avoid becoming infected when treating patients.

It is hoped that nanomedicine can aid in Ebola's elimination. Early detection of the disease has been difficult because many of its symptoms are very common. For example, fever is one early sign of Ebola. However, a fever could also just mean that a person is suffering from a common cold. It might take up to three days after the first symptoms arise to spot proof of Ebola. But nanomedicine researchers have created a device that detects the disease using one drop of blood from the patient.

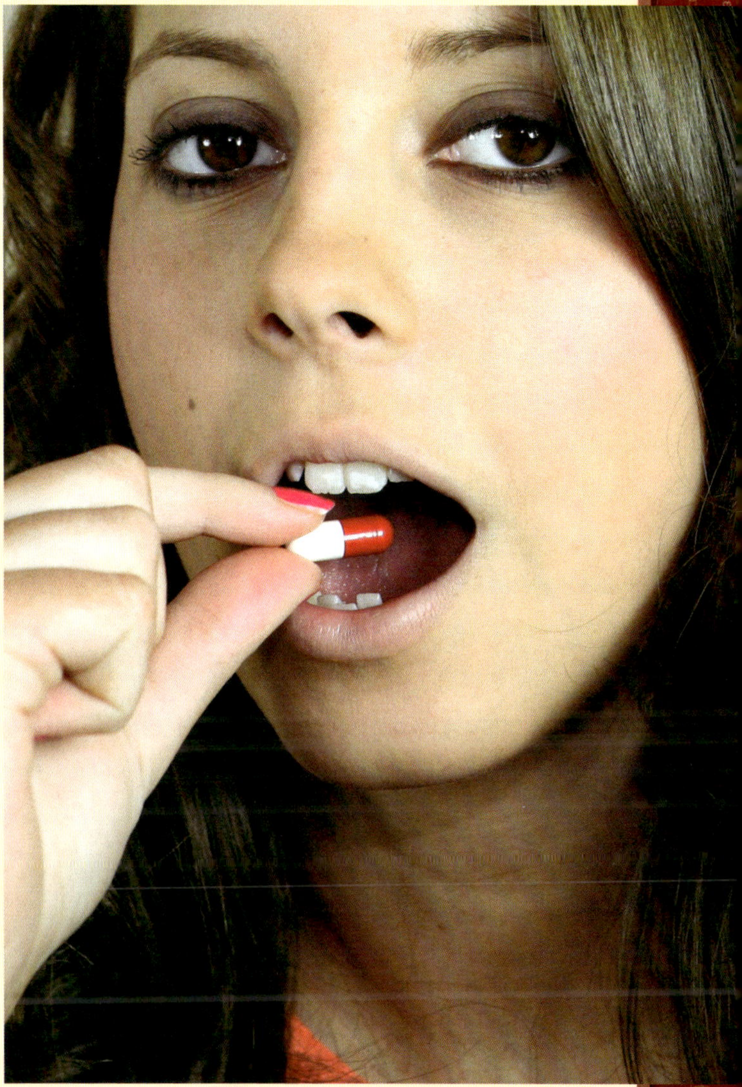

Overuse of antibiotics has made drug-resistant bacterias stronger. When antibiotics kill weaker bacterias, drug-resistant bacterias are left to grow and multiply.

Bacteria that resist antibiotics have also become a growing problem. This has made it more difficult to keep some diseases from spreading. This is especially true in developing countries with poor health care systems. The result is a global threat. Only through early detection and treatment can such deadly illnesses be controlled. Nanomedicine will help lead that fight.

Tracking Down Disease

A disease cannot be eliminated if it cannot be found. Perhaps the most important benefit of nanomedicine is its potential to diagnose problems before they become serious. Nanomedicine can scope out the causes of new diseases. It could restore vision before it weakens. It could identify and monitor mental illnesses. Advances could lead to extended life spans in humans and animals.

Researchers have used **antibodies** attached to carbon nanotube carriers to detect cancer cells in the bloodstream. In lab tests, these sensors have shown evidence of being able to provide detection that could save lives. Sensors might be used to spot cancer growth at its earliest stage. They could potentially find as few as three cancer cells in a tiny blood sample.

Antibodies are Y-shaped proteins produced by the immune system to attack disease-causing bacteria or viruses.

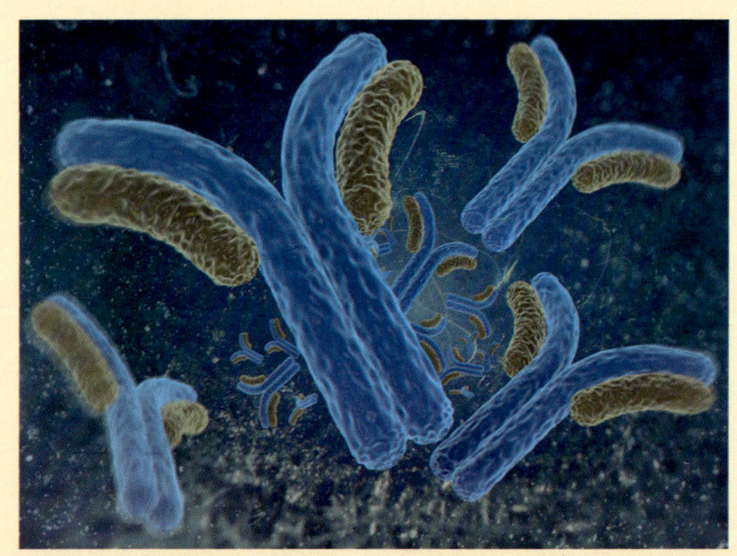

Tests have given hope that other illnesses can also be diagnosed quickly through similar methods. Carbon nanotube sensors in gel form can be injected under the skin to monitor the level of nitrous oxide in the bloodstream. This level is important because it indicates inflammation, which is a symptom of diseases such as arthritis. Research shows that the sensors can remain functional inside the body for more than a year.

Early diagnosis of infectious diseases has also been proven possible. Scientists have demonstrated the use of nanoparticles attached to molecules in the bloodstream to show the start of an infection.

The Downsides of Nanomedicine

Nanomedicine is not without its risks. For example, what if nanoparticles became permanently stuck in a patient's body? This could potentially cause a variety of health issues. Nanomedicine could also cause problems beyond the patients it is used on. Some have warned that the use and disposal of nanoparticles could harm the environment. Nanomedicine's high cost could lead to unfairness. Some believe that only the rich will be able to afford the latest treatments, leaving poorer people on the outside looking in. Will everyone who needs nanomedicine have equal access to it? Such issues might not be worked out before nanomedicine has been cleared for widespread use. Its potential to save lives could prove too powerful to wait for proper regulations to be in place.

Researchers have developed gold nanorods, which possess unique detection properties. They are attached to protein produced by damaged kidneys. The color of the nanorod changes as the protein builds up. This quick and inexpensive test allows for the early detection of potentially deadly kidney disease.

Even serious physical injuries might soon be treated using nanomedicine. For example, car crashes often damage the body to the point where it cannot be treated. But nanotechnology might come to the rescue. Permanent nanorobots embedded in a tissue can strengthen it against tearing or even repair it once it is torn. A blow to the head can rattle the brain against the skull. But a nanodevice, implanted prior, could cushion the brain and prevent damage.

Nanomedicine could help athletes, such as football players, repair torn muscles while they are playing. Nanorobots inside the body would use atoms and molecules inside the body to repair damaged tissue in real-time.

Some experts predict that nanomedicine will eliminate nearly all common diseases and the pain they cause by 2050. Researchers also forecast the elimination of drug resistance. Scientists also predict that nanomedicine could greatly increase the average person's life span. People would be much more likely to die of old age than of disease or injury. This is where some believe that science might be going too far. Everyone likes the idea of eliminating disease and pain to improve quality of life. But not everyone embraces the notion that life should be extended endlessly. Eliminating diseases and other natural causes of death would make the world more crowded.

Nanomedicine could also extend beyond life on Earth. It has been suggested that it could make long-distance space travel possible. Fitting space suits with technology that could diagnose and treat illnesses in astronauts would allow them to remain in space for prolonged periods of time. As space travelers will explore the universe, scientists will explore nanomedicine. The two scientific journeys seem destined to go hand in hand.

NASA is working on a nanotechnology coating to allow spacesuit batteries to last longer in temperatures ranging from **-148° Fahrenheit to 212°F** (-100° Celsius to 100°C).

Nanoparticles can be **30 Times** more effective at killing drug-resistant **bacteria** than traditional antibiotics.

Nanomedicine Timeline

Before microscopes were able to see individual atoms and molecules, scientists were theorizing about the potential benefits of nanomedicine. With the introduction of modern technology throughout the 20th century, scientists have discovered practical applications for nanotechnology in many fields including medicine.

1857

Michael Faraday discovers that nanostructure gold, under certain lighting conditions, produces different-colored solutions.

1959

Richard Feynman gives the first lecture on technology and engineering at the atomic scale at the California Institute of Technology.

1981

Gerd Binnig and Heinrich Rohrer invent the scanning tunneling microscope, allowing scientists to see individual atoms for the first time.

Doctors have discovered new ways of using nanomedicine to help deliver drugs throughout the body, to monitoring the health of a patient. In the future, it is believed that nanomedicine will extend the human life span considerably.

1991

Sumio Iijima discovers the carbon nanotube. It can be used by doctors to grow bone cells.

2005

The anti-cancer drug Abraxane uses nanoparticles, replacing the need of using toxins in an older form of the drug. Researchers discover that dangerous metals required in some medications can be replaced by nanoparticles.

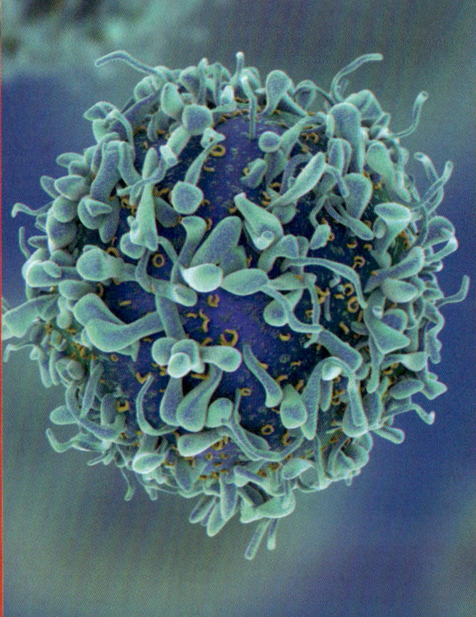

2018

Dr. Jelena Janjic creates the first inflammatory pain nanomedicine that targets specific locations in the body. With this treatment, about 2,000 times less medicine is needed.

Quiz

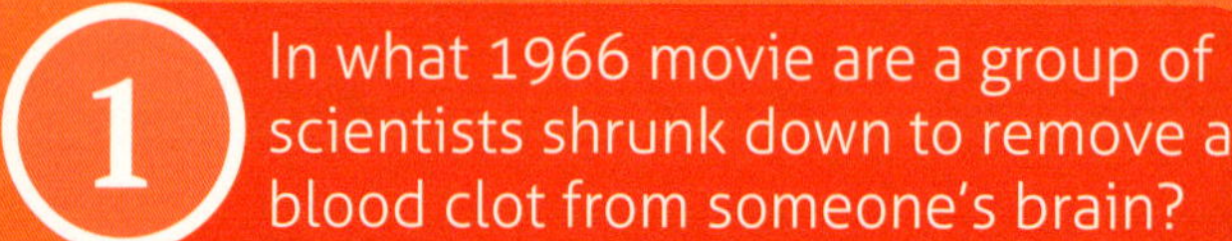

1. In what 1966 movie are a group of scientists shrunk down to remove a blood clot from someone's brain?

2. What larger field is nanomedicine a part of?

3. In 1959, who predicted that atoms and molecules would be manipulated one by one using precise instruments?

4. What could be placed into a patient's bloodstream to spot cancer cells at an early stage?

5. What is the name of a carbon molecule shaped like a soccer ball?

6. What is an emotional disorder that causes people to develop an obsessive desire to lose weight?

7. Which disease could be treated using nanoparticles carrying insulin?

8. What is a physical fence made of cells protecting the brain from harmful substances in the blood called?

9. What do researchers attach to carbon nanotube carriers to detect cancer cells in the bloodstream?

10. By what year do some experts predict that nanomedicine will eliminate nearly all common diseases and the pain they cause?

Answers: **1.** *Fantastic Voyage* **2.** Nanotechnology **3.** Richard Feynman **4.** A carbon nanotube **5.** Buckyball **6.** Anorexia **7.** Diabetes **8.** The blood-brain barrier **9.** Antibodies **10.** 2050

Key Words

antibodies: substances produced by the body to fight disease

atoms: the tiniest parts of an element that have all the properties of that element

bacterial: of or relating to bacteria, which are microscopic, single-celled organisms that exist everywhere and can be either helpful or harmful

chemotherapy: use of chemicals to kill diseased cells in cancer patients

infectious: easily passed from one person to another

inflammation: redness, swelling, heat, and pain caused by disease or injury

insulin: a substance made by the body that controls blood sugar levels

molecules: the smallest amounts of a chemical compound that still display all of its chemical properties

radiation: energy emitted from a radioactive substance in the form of atomic particles or waves

toxins: poisonous substances produced by a living thing

tumors: masses of abnormal cell tissue found in or on the body

Index

LIGHTBOX

SUPPLEMENTARY RESOURCES

Click on the plus icon found in the bottom left corner of each spread to open additional teacher resources.

- Download and print the book's quizzes and activities
- Access curriculum correlations
- Explore additional web applications that enhance the Lightbox experience

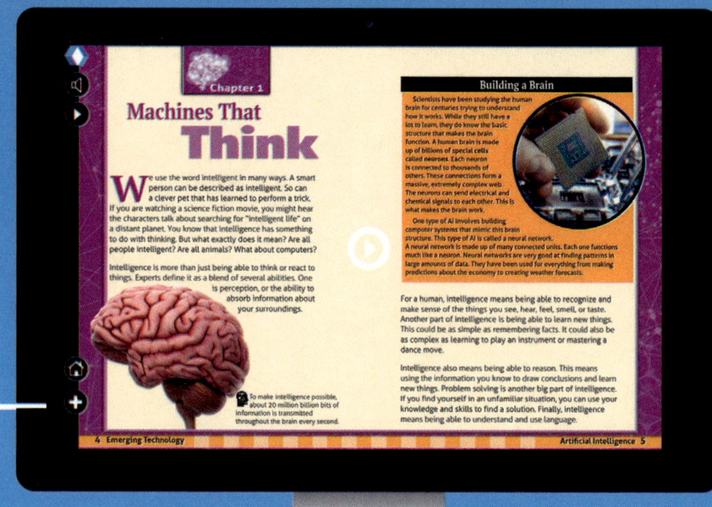

LIGHTBOX DIGITAL TITLES

Packed full of integrated media

VIDEOS

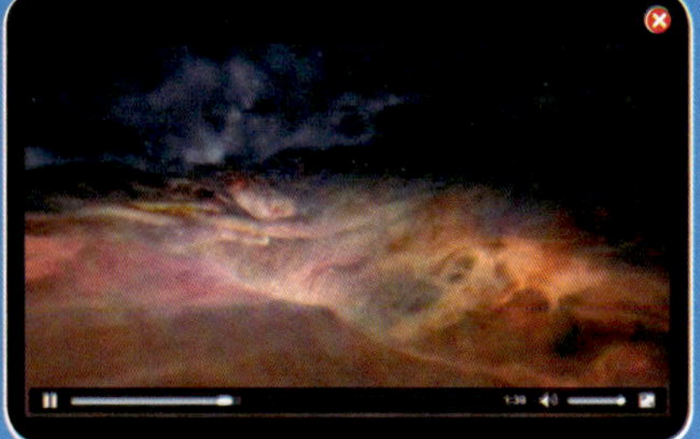

INTERACTIVE MAPS

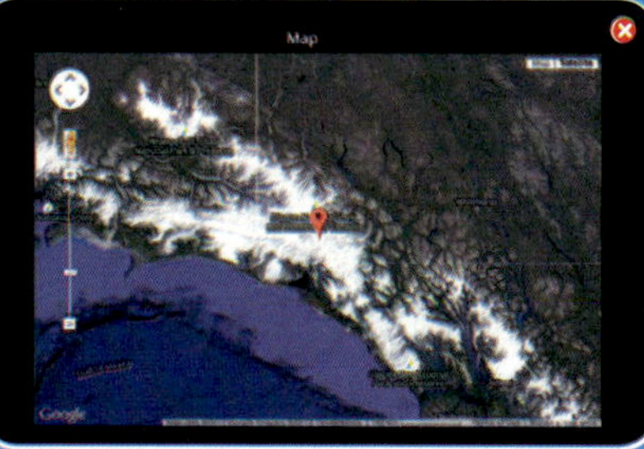

WEBLINKS

SLIDESHOWS

QUIZZES

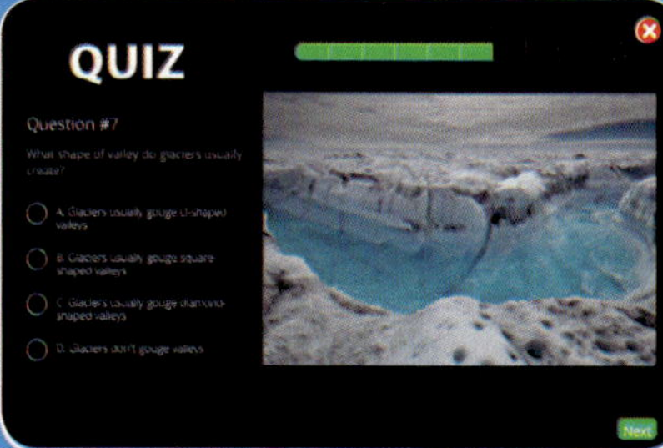

OPTIMIZED FOR

- ✓ TABLETS
- ✓ WHITEBOARDS
- ✓ COMPUTERS
- ✓ AND MUCH MORE!

Published by Smartbook Media Inc.
350 5th Avenue, 59th Floor
New York, NY 10118
Website: www.openlightbox.com

Library of Congress Control Number: 2018930329

ISBN 978-1-5105-3932-7 (hardcover)
ISBN 978-1-5105-3931-0 (multi-user eBook)

Printed in Brainerd, Minnesota, United States
1 2 3 4 5 6 7 8 9 0 22 21 20 19 18

052018
110117

Project Coordinator Jared Siemens
Designer Ana María Vidal

Photo Credits
Every reasonable effort has been made to trace ownership and to obtain permission to reprint copyright material. The publisher would be pleased to have any errors or omissions brought to its attention so that they may be corrected in subsequent printings. The publisher acknowledges Getty Images, Newscom, iStock, Shutterstock, and Alamy as its primary image suppliers for this title.